FOUR E.S.T. MARATHON '99

ALL ABOUT AL BY CHERIE VOGELSTEIN
DEAF DAY BY LESLIE AYVAZIAN
DREAMTIME FOR ALICE BY SUSAN KIM
GOODBYE OSCAR BY ROMULUS LINNEY

★

DRAMATISTS
PLAY SERVICE
INC.

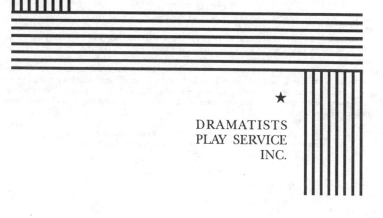

TABLE OF CONTENTS

ALL ABOUT AL

BY

CHERIE VOGELSTEIN

ALL ABOUT AL was produced by The Ensemble Studio Theatre (Curt Dempster, Artistic Director) at their Marathon '99, 22nd Annual Festival of New One-Act Plays, in New York City in May 1999. It was directed by Jamie Richards; the set design was by Kris Stone; the costume design was by Amela Baksic; the lighting design was by Greg MacPherson; the sound design was by Beatrice Terry; and the production stage manager was Gretchen Knowlton. The cast was as follows:

GIL . . . . Mark Giordano
LENNY . . . . Mark Feuerstein
AL . . . . Jennifer Carta
COFFEE BAR CUSTOMER . . . . JC Cassano

ALL ABOUT AL

Gil, very handsome and cool, sits with his back to us in an empty coffee shop, reads the sports section. Lenny, downtrodden and uncool, enters in raincoat and galoshes, furtively looks around, spots Gil, quickly looks away, orders coffee. Nonchalantly, Lenny takes cup and saunters by Gil's table. Suddenly, he stops, pretends to notice Gil for the first time.

Their initial conversation should be slightly awkward: the way it is when casual friends meet after not speaking for a while; full of sound and excitement, signifying nothing.

LENNY.   Gil! *(Practically spills cup.)*

GIL.   *(Looks up.)* Hey ... Lenny —

LENNY.   What a surprise, what a coincidence!

GIL.   Yehah — how ya doin', buddy?

LENNY.   How are *you?* You look great!

GIL.   Yeah? Well, I'm doin' OK, you know, hangin' in there ... *(Awkward pause, then with some concern.)* ... how uh ... how are YOU doin', Len?

LENNY.   *(Jovially.)* Me? Well, I'm fine — all right, you know — not so good — *(Totally serious.)* — suicidal, Gil — I'm suicidal.

GIL.   *(Sympathetic.)* Yeah, heard about you and Cindy. I'm sorry, man, we shoulda called.

LENNY.   No, no *I* should've called you guys ... it's just I've been so preoccupied, you know, with death, I haven't had any time. *(Cheery.)* So how's Allison?

GIL.   Allison? She's real good ... yeah, she should be comin' here —

LENNY.   *(Excited.)* Really?!

GIL.   Yeah.

LENNY.   Here? Really? *(Gil nods.)* That's great, that is so great!

GIL.   *(Puzzled by Lenny's enthusiasm.)* Yeah ... any minute.

LENNY.   *(Elated.)* I — I can't wait to see her, I mean what good luck ... that is so fantastic, just terrific ... incredible really ...

GIL.   *(Beat.)* You're not gettin' out much, are ya, Len?

LENNY.   *(Instantly sad, sits, cradles his head.)* It's hopeless, Gil. I'm miserable, A WRECK: all alone during allergy season with my hair falling out and my gums big and bleeding — may I join you? —

GIL.   *(Looks around uncomfortably.)* Uh —

LENNY.   — I mean you don't know how lucky you are — wow — to have a woman like Allison, kind, darling, beautiful Al —

GIL.   Len —

LENNY.   *(Raptured.)* Oh God, God, I love her like a — *(Realizes.)* — a relative, a sister — *(Has to be honest.)* — a stepsister —

GIL.   Yeah, I know —

LENNY.   — but she's the last of her species, there are no Allisons left in this world — I thought Cindy might be an Allison, but she too turned into a Tina and I — *(He farts, looks up at Gil in shocked horror.)* — oh that is just inexcusable Gil — I don't know what to say —

GIL.   It's all right — Lenny listen — *(They speak at the same time.)*

LENNY.   — ever since Cindy left, my gastrointestinal tract —

GIL.   — I have to tell ya somethin' —

LENNY.   — it has a mind of its own ... I oughta kill myself —

GIL.   — when Allison gets here —

LENNY.   — and I will — unless I find a woman —

GIL.   — I think we're breakin' up.

LENNY.   *(Shocked.)* What?

GIL.   *(Beat.)* Yeah.

LENNY.   *(Devastated beat.)* No.

GIL.   *(Beat.)* Yeah ...

LENNY.   *(Beat.)* No.

GIL.   Yeah.

LENNY.   *(Two beats.)* No.

GIL.   *(Annoyed.)* LENNY —

LENNY.   I'm sorry but I ... can't believe it ... I mean I just can't believe it — you and Allison, Allison and you ... you're like Romeo and Juliet ... Antony and Cleopatra ... Laurence Olivier and Danny Kaye —

GIL. *(With distaste.)* Oh man ...

LENNY. I'm just so shocked — I'm in shock — wow — *(Shakes his head, louder.)* — wowza — *(Loud, smiling.)* — WOWZA!

GIL. Well listen ... I'm just tellin' ya cuz maybe, you know, it's not such a good idea for you to be around when I tell her —

LENNY. Why, Gil? I'll be very quiet —

GIL. Right but uh ... even though it's a cafe deal and I'm hopin' she'll keep the cryin' violent shit down to a minimum ... I'll tell ya, Len, things might get pretty wacky — I mean, it's not easy breakin' a girl's heart ... ya know?

LENNY. No ... I don't know ... I've dreamt about it ...

GIL. Yeah well so anyway ... I think that's what I'm gonna do. *(Pause.)*

LENNY. But can you just tell me, Gil, why? I mean ... why? Why?

GIL. What're ya askin' me?

LENNY. Well uh ... *(Beat, a tad perplexed.)* I guess I'm asking you why.

GIL. But now see, how can I answer somethin' like that? I mean ... there're about four million reasons and no reasons at all except some voice inside ya says it's gotta be done and you can't track down why. It's from a place of no logic it's not about logic it's bigger than logic. It's bigger than you. So you listen. *(Beat.)* Cuz once you stop listenin', once you stop, Lenny ... you're lost. You got no voices left.

LENNY. *(Beat.)* Are you shtupping someone else?

GIL. *(Immediate.)* Yeah.

LENNY. *(Horrified.)* Are you really?

GIL. *(Laughs.)* Hey gimme a break, will ya? It's nothin' like that —

LENNY. So then what is it, Gil? Really. I want to know. I mean, I REALLY NEED to know! Everybody says they're looking for love, looking for love, looking for love, and what do they do the minute they get it? They flush it away — flush, flush, flush! *(Furious.)* This world is just one vast toilet of devotion, one big bathroom of romance where it's better coming out than it was going in — I'm sick of it I tell you, SICK! So listen to *this* voice,

Gil, and listen good: You're not breaking up with Allison unless you have a damn good reason for it, a damn good reason! Do you hear me, Gil? Do you hear me? *(Yells.)* DO YOU HEAR ME?

GIL. *(Beat.)* Are you ... are you on some kind of medication, Leonard?

LENNY. *(Sits.)* Sinutab — I'm sorry, I'm sorry but *(Upset again.)* ... *you're* my friend too — *(Rises again.)* — I won't let you throw your life away! Sure, sure, I may know Allison longer but let's face it Gil — *we're* men — at least you are — and men have to look out for each other, care, bond, love — all right not love, love's too much but —

GIL. *(Genuine.)* Listen, I appreciate your concern, but uh you got your own problems there, buddy —

LENNY. Please, I can always take on more — I welcome it! Gil, don't deprive me of a vicarious thrill, Gil, it's all I have left — *(Gil is weakening.)* — if I can help you two work it through, if we can talk it out —

GIL. Well, ya know, maybe that's not such a bad idea cuz like, she's prob'ly gonna ask me why too, right? So maybe I oughta prepare (what I'm gonna say) —

LENNY. Yes, yes, you definitely should — wait — *(He turns away, ties napkin under his chin like a kerchief, turns to face Gil, speaks in falsetto.)* — now — hi, Gil, how are you? *(Gil looks perplexed.)*

GIL. What're you doin'?

LENNY. *(In falsetto.)* I'm Allison —

GIL. Oh! *(Laughs.)* No offense, Len, but you make a real ugly girl —

LENNY. *(Sticking to his role, falsetto.)* Did you want to speak to me about something —

GIL. OK, OK yeah ... *(Serious.)* ... I did ... listen, Al, I haveta tell you something —

LENNY. *(Coquettishly.)* I love you, Gilly —

GIL. Yeah, I love you too. It's over. We have to break up.

LENNY. What?! Why?!

GIL. Why? *(Thinks.)* Honestly? Because ... I have a brain tumor —

LENNY. *(Falsetto.)* Oh my God! You do?

GIL. No, no, no — seriously? We have to break up because ... I'm not good enough for you, Al, I think you deserve better —

LENNY. *(Falsetto.)* I do but I don't want better, I want you, YOU — *(Almost to himself.)* — moronic, greasy —

GIL. *(Oblivious.)* Yeah but the thing is ... I don't think I can measure up to this ... this IMAGE you havea me, ya know? I mean, sure we might be good today, we might be good tomorrow but ultimately, I don't have what it takes to fulfill a girl like you. And one day, one day I'm gonna look into your eyes and I'm gonna see — insteada the love — I'm gonna see somethin' else — I'm gonna see all the respect drained out and gone with only the hate left. And that's gonna break my heart, Al — *(Sobs.)* — it's gonna fuckin' break my Goddamn heart.

LENNY. *(As himself.)* Wow. Is that true?

GIL. No but it sounded good, right? *(Beat.)* I mean, you can't tell her the real shit, like ... like how you hate what she does in bed!

LENNY. What does she do in bed?

GIL. Oh, well, nothin', nothin', just ... ya know ...

LENNY. No I don't know — *(Casual.)* — I'm willing to know, I mean, I'd pay to know —

GIL. Well it's no big deal really, just this thing she does sometimes when ... when we're lyin' there ... ya know, after sex ... and I'll be gettin' all comfortable, I'll be startin' to doze off cuz like ... I'm FINISHED, right? — and allofa sudden, outta nowhere, I'll feel this leg swingin' over on top of me, right over my body while I'm tryin' to sleep —

LENNY. Is it *her* leg?

GIL. Of course it's her leg that's not the point — the point is while I'm tryin' to sleep, I don't need some weight pinnin' me down to the mattress, you know what I mean?

LENNY. Cindy bought a bunk bed when I moved in —

GIL. I mean, I'm not sayin' I don't appreciate Al's affection — I'm not saying that at all — but there's a time and a place and after sex ... I do NOT like to be touched, ya know?

LENNY. Cindy said even during, it should be kept to a minimum.

GIL. Yeah well Cindy was a pig —

LENNY. *(Defiantly.)* But she was my pig.

GIL. Listen, Len, can I just say? — she did you the biggest favor in the world when she dumped you —

11

LENNY. I know, I know. That's the one favor women always want to do for me — *(With sudden emotion.)* — which is why I'm telling you it's lonely in New York, Gil — Allison is special —

GIL. Yeah, I know she's special but ... but ... it's not just the leg thing, Lenny ... it's more than that ...

LENNY. You mean like a leg/arm kind of a thing?

GIL. I mean like ... like — *(Thinks of something.)* — like the way she's so obsessed with her weight! I mean, all she ever does is ask me about it all the time: Like I won't have seen her for a *day* and I'll pick her up and first thing when she opens the door, she'll say, "Hi Gil do I look like I gained weight?"

LENNY. So?

GIL. So I'll say — No, Al, you look great — and she'll say — are you sure? — and I'll say — positive — and she'll say — no you're lying — and I'll say — why would I lie? — to make me feel good — no, no way — yes, I see it in your eyes — no, that's my contact lens Al, ya haven't gained an ounce since the day you were born — you promise? — I swear — you'd tell me if I did — of course — you promise you would tell me? — I promise — you promise you promise — I promise, I swear, I swear on my fucking life now give me a Goddamn stake to put through my head cuz I can't take it anymore, Lenny, it drives me fuckin' nuts!

LENNY. Why? *(Gil rolls his eyes in frustration.)* You mean because she's a little insecure about her figure ... needs a little reassurance, a little positive assessment of her weight?

GIL. Yeah but like ... why doesn't she just invest inna fuckin' scale? Ya know what I mean? Why's it haveta be such a big fuckin' *mystery* all the time?

LENNY. Gil, Gil, YOU'RE her scale, Gil, YOU —

GIL. But that's the thing — to me she looks great — so what's she so worried about?

LENNY. *(Shrugging.)* Maybe she's afraid if she got fat, you'd break up with her.

GIL. Well, yeah ... I would — but that doesn't mean she has to like "dwell," ya know? *(Guiltily.)* I mean, come on, Len — every guy wants his girlfriend to have a nice body, right?

LENNY. *(Nodding.)* Cindy gained sixty pounds while we were

12

together.

GIL.   God, I know — how'd you deal with that, man?

LENNY.   I loved her for what was inside —

GIL.   *(Eating.)* Deep, deep inside —

LENNY.   *(Impassioned.)* Look, a good woman is hard to find —

GIL.   *(Still chewing.)* Cindy's not hard to find — *(Spreads his arms wide.)*

LENNY.   — Allison's not only beautiful inside AND out but she also —

GIL.   Swallows.

LENNY.   P-pardon?

GIL.   Yeah but ya know, don't mention it, like when she comes.

LENNY.   Listen, it's not an easy thing to weave into a conversation —

GIL.   *(Thoughtful.)* The truth is, I don't really give her enough credit for bein' so ... ya know, giving. I mean she's like a real tribute to her race — ahh, I shouldn't talk about this stuff, it's private shit. *(Beat.)*

LENNY.   Gil, I understand if you don't care to share this topic with me but let me just say I'd give my life to hear about it.

GIL.   *(Hesitates.)* Well ... all right, just between the two of us — *(Launches ahead.)* — what they say about Jewish girls is usually true, right? —

LENNY.   Wha — what do they say about Jewish girls?

GIL.   Ya know ... that they're not too big on givin' head —

LENNY.   Oh. I thought that was all girls —

GIL.   — yeah well I'm just sayin', especially Jewish girls, so like to find a Jewish girl who not only enjoys goin' down, but is also willing to ... imbibe — you're talkin' a rarity. *(Lenny clears his throat, chokes a little.)* Not to be, ya know, too crude —

LENNY.   *(Quickly.)* That's all right, that's fine —

GIL.   — but Al goes at it like a thirsty sailor on the hot Russian steppe and doesn't come up for air, ya know what I'm sayin'? — don't mention it, Len. Len?

LENNY.   *(Nodding, choking, takes out inhaler.)* I'm just ... I'm just having a little difficulty breathing. *(He uses inhaler.)*

GIL.   *(Looks around, then at his watch.)* I wonder why Al's so late.

13

LENNY.   Cindy was always late, Cindy —

GIL.   Cindy, Cindy, will you forget fuckin' Cindy!

LENNY.   It just ended last week, Gil.

GIL.   Yeah well get over it already, all right? Get over it!

LENNY.   *(Repeats to himself.)* Get over it.

GIL.   I mean, the girl treated you like total shit!

LENNY.   A little worse.

GIL.   Exactly! So just move on, ya know? Move on. You're free!

LENNY.   Free.

GIL.   Yeah, yeah — it's a guy's world, Len — I mean a sixty-year-old man can get a twenty-year-old girl — *(He snaps.)* — like that!

LENNY.   Really? *(He snaps.)* Like that?

GIL.   Nothin' to it.

LENNY.   So that's it, that's my problem? I'm too young?!

GIL.   No, no, you're too nice! You like these girls who walk all over ya —

LENNY.   I do, I'm grateful to them —

GIL.   — when what you need is somebody nice, somebody sweet, a girl who gives ya support, makes ya feel good, really LIKES you —

LENNY.   *(Like a kid at a toy store.)* They have that?

GIL.   Yeah, yeah, ya just gotta give yourself a break, buddy, ya know what I mean? Ya gotta ... go for it, ya know? *(Beat.)* Just go for it! *(Pause.)*

LENNY.   Gil?

GIL.   Yeah, Len?

LENNY.   When uh when Allison gets here ...

GIL.   Yeah?

LENNY.   When Allison gets here ...

GIL.   Yes?

LENNY.   When Allison gets here could I ... could I ...

GIL.   *(Very calm.)* Finish the fuckin' sentence, Len.

LENNY.   ... have her?

GIL.   What?

LENNY.   Well not "have her," "have her" is a silly expression but you know what I mean — could I ask her out — would you mind?

GIL.   Would I mind? If you asked Allison out?

14

LENNY. Yes, 'cuz you said —

GIL. You want to ask Allison out? *(Feigning complete calm.)*

LENNY. Well ... yes.

GIL. *(Beat.)* *My* Allison, right? You mean Allison Kramer.

LENNY. Listen, if it's a problem —

GIL. No, it's no problem —

LENNY. — then I won't —

GIL. It's no problem just —

LENNY. Just what?

GIL. Just nothin', nothin' ... it's fine.

LENNY. Are you sure? Because —

GIL. Lenny. I said it's not a problem, OK?

LENNY. OK. *(Beat, smiling broadly, happily.)* Thanks, Gilly.

GIL. Don't ever call me Gilly, all right? *(Beat, scowling.)* But I'm just thinkin' ...

LENNY. *(Serious.)* Uh-huh, good, OK —

GIL. Ya know ... what about "Cindy"?

LENNY. Oh. Well you said to forget her.

GIL. And that's it? That's all it takes — I say "forget her" and you're done?

LENNY. Well, Gil, I thought you gave me some very excellent advice and so I'm trying to follow up on it, is all —

GIL. Yeah, well, OK ... good. *(Takes out cigarette, thinks awhile.)* But I haveta tell ya, Len, maybe this is sicka me an' all, but it kinda does bother me, ya know?

LENNY. *(Holds up coffee cup.)* This is not decaf.

GIL. *(Annoyed and confused.)* I mean you askin' Allison out, I mean, cuz like ... here you are, and and like ... the body's still warm, ya know what I'm sayin'?

LENNY. Yes but in a way, isn't that better? *(Smiles broadly.)* Because that way she won't have time to mourn over the loss of you, because I'll be right there to console her —

GIL. *(Getting angrier.)* Yeah but what I'm sayin' is I don't really want you there to console her —

LENNY. But ... why, Gil? I mean, do you want to see her suffer?

GIL. Not at all. But I even more don't want to see her with *you* —

15

LENNY.   But that's not very fair, is it? I mean, here you don't want her anymore —

GIL.   I never said I didn't "WANT" her, Lenny —

LENNY.   Well, you said you were breaking up —

GIL.   I said I was thinkin' of breaking up — that the little, dancin' thought had walked my mind! But I mean I didn't realize that automatically gave YOU the green fuckin' light to pounce.

LENNY.   *(Frantically looks towards door.)* But you said —

GIL.   I said alotta things — because you asked me — as a FRIEND — what I was thinkin' so I — wait! Wait — is that what this whole gig has been about, Lenny, huh?

LENNY.   Gig? What gig? Please, Gil, I'm gigless —

GIL.   *(Rises, angry.)* All your concern for the what, why, why — were you just, ya know, circlin' the area till you could swoop down — like some little galosh-wearin' vulture —

LENNY.   *(Backing away.)* That's not a very flattering characterization, Gil —

GIL.   — and ... and what? Just feast on my leftovers?!

LENNY.   I'm kosher, Gil, please —

GIL.   I mean, God! you are somethin', man — you are really somethin' —

LENNY.   How can you say that? You know I'm not something —

GIL.   — and ... and I mean for Allison, no less — Allison of all girls — don't you know how outta your league Allison is?

LENNY.   Yes of course but — but you said to go for it!

GIL.   It. It. IT! Not HER, you asshole!

LENNY.   *(Summoning up his courage.)* But why not? *(Rises.)* Why not her?

GIL.   Because ... because —

LENNY.   *(Hitting his stride.)* Because what, Gil, HUH?! All my life I've watched the Leonards of this world lose the Allisons of this world to the Gils of this world and the Gils don't even care! They don't even fucking care!!! *(He throws Gil's coffee against wall.)* I'm sick of it I tell you — sick, sick, sick!

GIL.   *(Calmly immediate.)* That was my coffee.

LENNY.   *(Overlap.)* It's men like you who destroy women for the rest of us — abusing and demeaning and rejecting them till they so totally lose their sense of selves they actually believe the REAL men are the men who treat them that way — !

GIL. *(Shrugs.)* Yeah ...

LENNY. — when in fact you're not real at all, you're just scared, scared of growing up, scared of yourself, scared that — just like you said in that speech — that one day you're gonna look into her eyes and see the hate because deep down you believe once Allison sees you, once she really sees Gilly for who he is, she'll see THERE'S NOTHING TO SEE!

GIL. Yeah? *(Rises.)* Well — *(Trying to find the right words.)* — fuck you, Lenny! Fuck you! *(Screams, grabs his collar.)* FUCK YOU! *(Silence; Gil lets go.)*

LENNY. *(Beat.)* I think I've offended you Gil — *(Sits.)* — I'm sorry —

GIL. No, don't be sorry, don't be sorry — who wants your sorry, Lenny? I mean, you think I think Al's just some lay ... some ... some pop? Well you're wrong! Allison's a GIFT, a PRIZE — who loves me! And so that's a VERY scary thing — *(Lenny uses inhaler.)* — I mean, it's alotta pressure — alotta — who wants to deal with disappointin' a girl like that, ya know?! We're not talkin' some bitch whale beast like Cindy — we're talkin' Allison Kramer! And so even if a part athat — if part awhat you said — fear — whatever you said — even if it's something involved with that ... so what? I mean — what does that prove? That I'm no good, I'm shit? Because I'm — I'm human? That I may be scared of rejection deep down? All right! So what, ya know? Deep down everybody's scared of rejection! Everybody!

LENNY. *(Puffing up his chest.)* I'm not!

GIL. Yeah? Well that's just cuz you're so fuckin' used to it —

LENNY. Damn straight! Damn straight I am! *(Rises, speaks quietly.)* Take a look at a real man, Gil — a man who's not afraid of rejection, of intimacy, of commitment, the dark — well OK I am a little afraid of the dark — but I'm not afraid of love! Love I embrace unguarded — and I love Allison! I want her, Gil!

GIL. *(Also rises.)* Yeah well so do I!

LENNY. *(Face to face.)* Yeah? Well ... well ... step outside.

GIL. Why? *(Shakes his head.)* You wanna fight?

LENNY. No. I just want you to step outside — *(Al enters.)* — Al!

GIL. *(Whirls around to face her.)* AL!

AL. *(Coming over.)* Hi, hi — Lenny, what a surprise!

GIL. You're late —

AL. Oh I'm sorry, the rain —

LENNY. That's all right —

GIL. I was worried —

LENNY. So was I —

GIL. — cuz Lenny has to go —

AL. Oh no — do you really?

LENNY. No, not really —

GIL. *(At the same time.)* Yeah, he does — *(Beat.)* — you look great, Al —

AL. *(Almost shyly, loves this.)* Do I? You don't think I gained a little weight?

GIL. No, baby — *(Meaningful beat.)* — and it wouldn't matter if you did. *(They gaze into each other's eyes.)*

LENNY. *(Witnessing their passion.)* Actually, I really should be getting back ... you know, to my empty apartment ...

GIL. Here — *(Reaches towards Al.)* — let me hang up your coat — *(He helps her out of it, hugs her tenderly.)*

AL. *(Lovingly.)* Thanks, Gilly — *(Turns back to Lenny.)* — well Len, listen, we have to get together SOON —

LENNY. Yeah ... *(Sad.)* ... soon.

GIL. Soon. *(Loud and clear.)* We'll see ya, Lenny.

LENNY. Yeah. See ya. *(He extends hand to Gil; Gil hesitates a second, then shakes, smiles. Lenny turns mournfully to Al.)* Goodbye, Al. *(He turns, walks towards door as Gil leaves to hang up coat. When Gil is out of sight, Lenny turns back, gives Al the OK sign; she smiles huge, signs it back to him. He smiles back, turns around, seems very sad, leaves. Blackout.)*

END OF PLAY

PROPERTY LIST

Sports section of newspaper (GIL)
Coffee cup (LENNY)
Napkin (LENNY)
Inhaler (LENNY)
Watch (GIL)
Cigarette (GIL)
Saucer (LENNY)
Coat (AL)

SOUND EFFECTS

Fart

DEAF DAY

BY

LESLIE AYVAZIAN

*Deaf Day is dedicated to
Kaitlyn Kenney*

DEAF DAY was produced by The Ensemble Studio Theatre (Curt Dempster, Artistic Director) at their Marathon '99, 22nd Annual Festival of New One-Act Plays, in New York City in May 1999. It was directed by Leslie Ayvazian; the set design was by Kris Stone; the costume design was by Amela Baksic; the lighting design was by Greg MacPherson; the sound design was by Beatrice Terry; and the production stage manager was Gretchen Knowlton. It was performed by Kaitlyn Kenney.

SETTING

The set for DEAF DAY is very simple: a chair.
Maybe a footstool.
Perhaps some toys on the ground.

TIME

Early morning for first scene.
Early evening for second scene.

DEAF DAY can be performed by a deaf actor or a hearing actor, a woman or a man. The Sign Language must be authentic.

DEAF DAY

A deaf mother talking to a deaf child, who does not appear on stage. Spoken aloud in English and also in Sign Language.

Ok.
Ready?
Come on!
Sun's up, Day's here.
Let's go!
Rise and shine.
That means: "Get up and ... be happy!"
Come on.
Don't ignore me.

Look at me! Yes!

We have to practice English.
Yes. Today is a practice day.
Your teacher said.
So look at me. Look at me!

Put your hearing aids in. Yes!

Now!

Good.

Ok.
We're going to the playground.
No, not at Deaf School.
In the Park.
Yes, there will be hearing children there.

I don't know if there will be any deaf kids.
You can speak to the hearing children.
Yes, you can.
Sure, you can.

Remember the new boy on our Street? Roger!
Maybe we'll see new boy Roger and his Dog!
You can talk to them. Yes!
And to other kids too.

Yes, you can.

You stand in front of them.
Look directly in their faces.
If they look away, say: *(No Sign.)* "Could you please repeat that?"
(No Sign.) "Could you please repeat that?"
(With Sign.) Yes, you can!
Say: *(No Sign.)* "I can't hear you because I'm deaf."

(Continues aloud and with Sign.) Some will laugh.
Some won't laugh.
Talk to the ones who don't laugh.
Come on, honey.
Yes.
Put your shoes on.
Put your shoes on!
I'll put them on you!
Then sit down and put them on!
Sit down!
Now tie your shoes.
Good.
Ok.
Get up.
Get up!
Get up!
Look at me!
Don't turn your head away.
Come on.

Ok.

I'll wait ... *(She waits. She taps her foot.)*

Hi.

Yes, I'll stay in the park with you, of course.

I'll sit on the closest bench.

You can talk to me whenever you want.

People may watch you.

And some may think: "WOW! Look at this kid!

He knows two languages! How cool!"

Well, some will think, "WOW!"

Some might be stupid.

We will ignore the stupid ones.

Do we feel sorry for the stupid ones?

Nah.

We think they're stupid.

But, some people will see how wonderful you are.

And those people will want to talk to you.

So, watch their faces.

Read their lips.

If they walk away without telling you where they are going, don't be mad.

Hearing people talk with their backs to each other.

At those times, wave to me.

We will talk.

And then, we'll come home. Yes.

And you can be quiet for as long as you want to be quiet.

No voices. Quiet.

Quiet.

Ok.

You ready?

Hearing aids, turned on!

Eyes open!

Let's go!

No, we don't have to march.
We can walk slowly!
We can walk real slowly.
And we'll look at each other.
And we'll talk.
In Sign.

We'll talk.

I promise. *(Without Sign.)*

Good. *(Without Sign.)*
(Lights shift. Lights come up. It is the same day: evening. She speaks aloud and with Sign.)

Hey.
It's almost time for bed!
Yes it is!
And you have sleepy eyes.
Yes, yes, yes you do.
But first ...
Look at me, honey. *(Hits floor for his attention.)*

(In just Sign.) Look at me! Good.

(Continues aloud and with Sign.) Let's practice English before we go to bed.
Practice Day is nearly finished.

Watch my face.
Come on, watch.

Let's talk about the Park.

No. No Roger! No dog. No.

But the Seesaw! Yes!

That girl!
No, we don't know her name.
But you two were perfectly balanced!
You sat in the air at the same time!
That's very special.

But the slide. I know.
They pushed you down the slide.
They wanted you to go faster.
They said: "HEY! ... HEY!"

They didn't know that you couldn't hear them.
So, they pushed.
They pushed hard. I know.

It surprised you.
And it hurt you. I know.

They pushed you because they were frustrated with you.

But I think you can understand
Sure you can.
Think about your deaf friends at school.
When you want their attention, sometimes you grab
them. Sometimes you hit them. Sure you do.
Because you want them to look at you.
And you get frustrated. Yes you do!

So, next time, if the kids are waiting, you go fast!
Ok!
Go fast down that slide.
You kick butt!
Yes!

Then no one will push you.
And no one will laugh.

You need to be fast and quick, quick, quick.
Like a bunny.
Yes.
A fast bunny who kicks butt!
That's you!
Yes!
Right! Jackie Chan!

Ok. *(Jumps up and does Jackie Chan stance.)*

Jackie Chan!

Auhhhhhh! *(Does Tae Kwon-Do kick.)*

We are Jackie Chan! *(Another move.)*

But you have sleepy eyes!

Yes.

(Said in Korean, no Sign:) Cha-Ryut. Kyung-Net. *(Bows to him.)* Tae Kwon-Do.

(Back to Sign and English.) So get in bed, Jackie Chan!

And maybe, tomorrow we'll go to the Planetarium.

Or the Zoo?

Maybe the Park.
And you can get back in the saddle.

That means: When you ride a horse and fall off, you need to get back on the horse right away. So you don't feel scared.

Back in the saddle.

Back in the Park.
Back on the slide.

Ok?

Ok.

Now sleep, honey.
Sweet dreams. *(She waves.)* Sweet dreams.

(She leaves "his room" and sits. She waits. Then she gets back up and goes to his room. She sees he is still awake, but sleepy. She waves again. She leaves and goes back to her chair. She waits. Then she goes again and checks on him. He's asleep. She returns to her chair and sits. She breathes a sigh of relief. Beat. She notices he has walked into the room. She speaks aloud and in Sign.)

What's up?

Tomorrow?

Stay home?

All day?

No voices?

Quiet?

I'm thinking. *(She gets up and sits on the floor.)*

Ok.

Tomorrow.

Quiet.

I promise.

Yes.

(In just Sign.) Quiet. Quiet. I Promise.

(In Sign and aloud.) Good night.

(In just Sign.) Good night. *(She sits watching her son. Lights fade.)*

END OF PLAY

DREAMTIME FOR ALICE

BY

SUSAN KIM

DREAMTIME FOR ALICE was produced by The Ensemble Studio Theatre (Curt Dempster, Artistic Director) at their Marathon '99, 22nd Annual Festival of New One-Act Plays, in New York City in May 1999. It was directed by Richard Lichte; the set design was by Kenichi Toki; the costume design was by Amela Baksic; the lighting design was by Greg MacPherson; the sound design was by Beatrice Terry; and the production stage manager was Gretchen Knowlton. The cast was as follows:

ALICE .... Cecilia deWolf
ANNOUNCER .... Julie McKee

CHARACTERS

ANNOUNCER — bright, upbeat, female, Australian. The voice of professional tour guides and stewardesses everywhere.

ALICE — an upper-middle-class, educated, white or Asian woman in her mid-40s. She is brittle, assured, and glib on the surface, and full of rage, fear, and mollusk vulnerability underneath. She is hatless, in shorts, sandals, T-shirt, and blouse. She carries a painted cloth "dilly" bag.

SETTING

A modest tourist stop in Central Australia, in the outback, about seventy miles north of Alice Springs. It consists basically of a very minor kind of rock outcropping, a bit of which is visible upstage left.

PRODUCTION NOTE

There are unspecific shifts in time as the day lengthens and ends, to be indicated by lighting and sound cues.

DREAMTIME FOR ALICE

*In darkness, the sound of a lone didgeridoo. It cuts out abruptly.
The voice of a cheerful Australian female.*

ANNOUNCER.   Attention, ladies and gentlemen, boys and
girls — Cheryl here again, and we hope you're enjoying your
Outback Adventure Tour. We're about a hundred and twenty
kilometers outside of Alice Springs, winding around the Mac-
Donnell Range on our way to Ayers Rock. Your photo opportu-
nity is just about up, so please get back on board the bus; we'll
be continuing westward seventy-five kilometers to our next point
of interest, Corroboree Rock, where you can buy souvenirs, have
a cuppa tea, and most important, have that wee you've probably
been worrying about. And remember: Australia has the highest
skin cancer rates in the world, so keep your heads covered. *(The
sound of a bus roaring away. Lights up. A modest tourist stop in the
Australian outback. It is very bright, very hot. A minute overhang of
rock is U. Alice, a hatless American tourist, stands reading from an Australian guidebook, a camera around her neck.)*
ALICE.   "Dreaming. To aborigines, the state of knowledge that
relates all objects and beings to one another by a complex series
of myths. The dreamtime was the time of creation, when the
world was forged by powerful beings who still walk the outback,
controlling universal destiny." *(She glances around and checks her
guidebook again.)* According to the dreaming, every rock, every
tree, every creature has a place in the cosmic order and a reason
for being. That boulder. The clouds. Every living thing. We are
all accounted for. We all have a place in the dreaming. *(Slaps at
an insect on her leg.)*
 The reason I'm here in the Australian outback is because I
am forty-three years old and I've never had an adventure. Not
once. Not unless you include fourteen years of marriage to a

psychopath. *(She lifts her camera and gazes through it around her, as if through binoculars.)*

I don't have much to say about Stan except that I have the distinct feeling he's *not* accounted for in the dreaming. When he wasn't telling loud, unfunny jokes or getting into screaming fights with strangers, he'd be tossing down gimlets and margaritas and stingers and punching things around me. Never me directly, but always something *next* to me. Walls, mirrors, the refrigerator. The air. For years, I actually thought this meant there wasn't a problem.

Anyway, that's enough about Stan. I'm here because he's not. I'm here to enjoy myself and forget all about him. *(A beat.)*

All right. What happened was, last Tuesday, Stan and I had "words" as the saying goes, and it came out that Stan has, *quel surpris*, a girlfriend. He's been seeing her for over a year, someone I actually know, our accountant Sorrel — and he informed me that not only were they madly in love, but that the two of them were flying to Impruneta for three weeks. In Tuscany. In Italy.

So what do you do at moments like that? Well, what are your options? Do you "A," fly into an unattractive rage? "B," wait it out, since it's only sex, and how long can that last, anyway? Or do you simply "C" — walk away from fourteen years, a life, a home, the whole ball of wax?

I don't know. I honestly don't.

All I knew was that I needed distance, space, and anonymity. So forty-eight hours later, give or take, I too was winging my way to a foreign country. To Alice Springs, Australia. Seeing as my name is Alice, it seemed only ... *(She notices something.)* Oh my God. *(She shades her eyes.)*

Oh, my God, it's a *dingo*, Mrs. Schwartzbaum? It's a real live dingo, come quick before it gets away!

And bring your camera! It's in that clump of bushes, it's yellow, and ... oh my God, it's got something in his mouth. It's got a *baby* in its mouth! Just kidding, Mrs. Schwartzbaum. Mrs. Schwartzbaum? *(She looks offstage.)* That's funny ... she was right behind me ... *(She walks offstage.)* Hello? Anybody? HELLLLO! *(A beat. She walks back on.)* Huh. *(She crosses off the other direction.*

Pause. She crosses back on.) Don't you just hate this kind of crap? *(She looks at her watch.)*

I hate to say it. I really hate to say it, but do you know what's going through my mind? I think she did it on purpose. That bitch, Cheryl. Why I don't know, but you don't just *leave* someone in the outback. You don't just leave an American *citizen* in the middle of the freaking *desert.* Vicious, passive-aggressive Australian *cow ... (She shades her eyes, looking off.)*

Sorry. Hostility alert. My therapist says I have "hostility issues." Meaning I spent so many years *not* expressing anger that it's finally gotten to the point where I honestly feel I don't have any, which even *I* know can't be true, only lately it's been starting to build up and occasionally spurt out in totally inappropriate ways and at the oddest people. Isn't it funny how you don't even have to have kids to turn into your own mother?

I don't think everyone is out to get me, by the way. I actually made a friend on the bus. Mrs. Schwartzbaum? She's this very charming, incredibly dapper little woman from Berlin. You'd think she might be wondering where I was, unless of course we hadn't hit it off as much as I thought. Which seems to be a recurrent theme in my life, as I've recently discovered. *(A boat. She takes out a compact and powders her nose.)*

One may be wondering if I'm starting to panic. I'm not. I'm an American tourist, you don't just lose an American tourist like that. At least not with the dollar the way it is these days. Besides, I'm all set. See? *(She rummages through her bag and takes out a small bottle of spring water, a food bar, and a Swiss army knife.)* Look — this one not only has the saw attachment but the little corkscrew, as well. If I run into any aborigine sommeliers, I'm all set. Once a Wellesley girl, always a Wellesley girl. *(Puts them away.)*

Anyway, I expect Cheryl will be realizing her mistake any second now. I expect that big gray bus will come roaring back down the road, and let me tell you one thing, I'm writing one very nasty letter to Outback Adventure Tours as soon as I get back to my room. *(Notices something off.)*

Oh, Christ.

All right, that's enough. Shoo! Go on! *(Stamps her foot.)* Some of the local fauna are mildly interesting, but only at a distance.

An *extreme* distance, I might add. *(To animal.)* That especially goes for lizards. I bet you're incredibly poisonous, aren't you? Nasty thing. *(Claps her hands.)* Now beat it! Go on. *(She notices her arm and examines it for sunburn.)*

Oh crap. Now what? *(She pokes her arm. She glances around and notices the tiny outcropping of rock. She stands under it. It provides virtually no cover whatsoever.)*

I just worry about this sun. It really is true that you can't appreciate how intense it is because it's so dry out here, and God knows the last thing I want is any more wrinkles. Some people are very proud about getting older, they say they don't mind all those little dings and dents and scars you accumulate over the years, but my feeling is, they're lying. As for me, I'm holding on as long as I ... *(Notices something off. In a whisper.)* Oh my good God Jesus Christ, would you look at that.

Parrots. *Hundreds* of them. Turquoise blue like the Caribbean sea, speaking of my least favorite island chain in the world. *(In her regular voice.)* All right ... that's enough. Move along now. Go on! *(Claps her hands. They take off.)* It's like some kind of *freak* show around here.

Anyway — about the sun? Epidermally speaking, this kind of sun is a killer. Have you ever been to New Mexico and just taken a look at the people who live there? They're like handbags with legs. I'm not making this up. My uncle lived in Albuquerque, and by the time he was 60, he had melanomas the size of silver dollars all over his entire body. He looked like a package of Wonder Bread. And of course I didn't bring a hat because I didn't think I'd be getting out of the Goddamn bus. *(Cocks her head.)*

Is that them? No? Christ, what am I, invisible? Do I make so little impression? How is it possible that not a single person on that entire bus notices I'm not around anymore?

Jesus. (Takes out a bottle of sunscreen and starts applying it to her face and arms.)

You see, I'm secretly very vain about my skin. That sounds silly, doesn't it. I mean, skin, big deal, what's to be proud of, right? It's not like having a beautiful face or endless legs or a massive set of knockers. None of which I have, as you may have already noticed. And if you haven't, just ask my husband. But for years — and this is the God's truth — my skin has been as soft as it was when I was a little girl. And when Stan and I first started dating, he used to touch me so gently, just with the tips of his fingers, as if he couldn't believe that underneath all the clothes and words and *things* on top, I could be so ... well, trust me. It's always been my best feature. *(She finishes and puts it away. Indicates her painted cloth bag.)*

I just bought this at the airport gift shop in Sydney. It's called a "dilly bag." If Stan were here, he'd probably say something like, "It's a real dilly, all right, Alice. You really know how to pick 'em."

I wish I had my hat with me. *(She takes her outer blouse and ties it on her head. It is very hot. Lights shift. Lights up. Alice sits reading her guidebook and eating her Power Bar.)*

Well, that's very interesting.

This is the story about the creation of Uluru ... "Uluru" being the aboriginal name for Ayers Rock, for anyone who gives a rat's ass. According to myth, Uluru was initially created by two little boys at play, and then it was subsequently molded by all the desert animals who lived nearby. Like the poisonous snake and the devil dingo.

"The devil dingo."

Now I don't know about anyone else, but I find that oddly charming. *(She fans herself with the book, licking her lips.)*

Jesus, my throat. I feel like I've swallowed a Fair Isle sweater. I think it's time for a little visit to the bar, don't you? *(Takes out her water.)*

Don't worry ... I'm only allowing myself a sip at a time. I shall drink sparingly, as of the blood of Christ. *(She takes a sip. It is rather longer than it should be. As she drinks, she notices something on the rock next to her. She screams, spilling some water as she jumps up. Claps her hands.)*

All right. Beat it! C'mon ... get lost! *(Takes off a sandal and considers smashing whatever it is ... but it escapes.)* Goddamn spiders. *(Recaps the bottle and puts it away.)*

One may be wondering why I chose Australia in the first place. I'm clearly not too keen on wildlife, or heat, or an entire nation of people descended from felons, come to think of it ...

41

so why Australia? Why not someplace *normal*, like ... Europe? Excluding Tuscany, of course. Well, I'll tell you why not Europe, there are too many Goddamn churches. I'm serious.

Well then, why the outback? Why this unintentional walkabout? Not that I'm actually *walking*, here, and not that I know what a walkabout is, exactly. A person ... walking about, I suppose. But that's what I like about all this, you see. How mysterious it is. How *weird*. Sere and lifeless like it's been scorched by a meteor. Because this ... *(Indicates horizon.)* ... all this is exactly how I look on the inside. Minus the parrots. See, for all its weirdness and otherness ... I feel like I *know* this place in some funny way, I fit in somehow, like I was here in a previous life. Or if I don't fit in, I could somehow. If only I could figure out how. And what would that bring me? Some kind of epiphany, I suppose? Some kind of answer?

Well, all right, then. The real reason is, I haven't done much traveling in my life, certainly not by myself, and it frankly makes me a little nervous. The only place a certain person would go to was the Caribbean. And don't ask which island, they're all essentially the same, and besides which it doesn't matter, we went to all of them. Which makes the Tuscan villa a little hard to digest.

Anyway ... the bottom line is, I wanted to go as literally and physically as far as I could from Englewood Cliffs — to the *antipodes* of New Jersey — and still be able to speak English. I know ... small of me, isn't it? Because the English language is my crutch. That much I'm not ashamed to admit, I'm an editor at a midsized publishing house, and a voracious reader and occasional writer, and words are what I do for a living. They're what I consider ... *(She notices something.)* Oh, thank Christ, it's about frigging time.

Jesus God in heaven, thank you, thank you mother Mary, Mama's goin' home ... *(She jumps up and runs D., waving.)* Hello! Over here! Hellooo! *(She slowly stops. She squints, rubbing her eyes. She laughs.)*

Well, talk about dubious accomplishments — I've had my first hallucination. But Jesus Christ, I could have sworn ...

I'm not religious, by the way. I know I mention God and Christ an awful lot, it may even look like I'm trying to petition them, but believe me, I'm not. The words just blip out of me sometimes, like ... religious Tourette's. Of course if your parents dragged you to church every Sunday for eighteen years, you'd know what I was talking about. It imprints on your brain in a very sinister way. Part of it always stays with you, like a vestigial ... flipper. *(Goes back to the rock. She opens her knife.)* Actually, that's not completely true, is it? *(Begins to carve in the rock.)*

I can honestly say I don't believe in God, and never did ... but wasn't there a time I was willing to give him a chance? What was I, eleven? Twelve? I had this friend, Mary. Mary Chaney. She went to Quaker meeting every Sunday with her family, and one day she asked if I wanted to go with them. So I did, and the only thing I remember was that this really old guy, although of course in retrospect he was probably like *thirty*, stood up, and said, "We are not here to speak to God. We are here for God to speak to us." Aha, I thought. So I sat there, very patiently, and waited for God to speak to me. I waited and waited and waited, and guess what, He didn't. Or if He did, He certainly didn't introduce himself. So needless to say, after an hour had gone by, I stopped waiting for Him. And eventually I stopped waiting altogether. *(Stands back to admire her work a moment: the word "Alice." Then she continues carving.)*

I know it looks like I'm defacing an aboriginal shrine here, but to be honest, I really don't give a shit. Besides, I think I've earned the right to let people know I was here. How else will my children be able to pinpoint where the scrappy old matriarch was lost before she was finally rescued?

I'm being figurative, by the way, I don't actually *have* any children. Stan again, of course. He never said no definitively, it was always the final bargaining chip, the last manipulative ploy in any argument we were having. How can we possibly have kids if you "fill in the blank"? "Take that job?" "Don't trust me with our finances?" "Hang over my head all the time like a freaking harpy?" I don't know, maybe it was for the best. Yeah ... like No shit Sherlock. But it's the single thing in fourteen years I almost left him over. And I never did. And now, of course, it's too late, I'm too, umm ... *(Licks her lips.)*

Christ, if only I had more water. Maybe I can just wet my whistle. Maybe I can just rinse out my mouth with water and then spit it back in the bottle. *(Undoes the bottle. She empties the contents into her mouth and swishes it around.)* Mmmmmmmmmmmm. *(She swallows. Wiping her mouth:)* Someone will be here soon. I know someone will be here very soon. *(Empties the final drops into her mouth and continues carving. Lights shift. Lights up. The words "Alice was here" are carved in the rock. Alice draws in the dirt with a pebble.)*

Try to remember. How far is it from here back to town? What did she say? Fifty kilometers? A hundred? So how much is that in miles? A ten-K road race is a little over six miles, so a *hundred*-K is sixty miles plus. If I wait until the sun sets, how long would it take me to run back to town?

Christ, who am I kidding?

But it's a choice. At least I have some autonomy, here. What if I were to travel *half* the distance? I could walk thirty miles, couldn't I?

Well ... what if I were to divide that in half?

And what if I were to divide that in half?

And then that in half?

Jesus, that's very interesting. When would it ever end?

It wouldn't, would it.

Because mathematically speaking, if you kept dividing a distance in half — over and over, to the minutest subatomic level — there are always an infinite number of points between two places — between here and civilization.

But that's just an intellectual construct. I'm just freaking myself out by breaking it down like that. What's that called again? Something-something-or-other? "How can you travel over an infinite series of points in a finite amount of time?" Zeno's paradox. So what was the answer?

The answer is, you can't.

Screw it all, of course you can. The reality is, you just do it. You just step forward.

So step forward.

Come on, Alice ... do something. Spring, Alice. See Alice spring. Spring, Alice, spring. *(She doesn't move. Lights shift. Lights up. Alice is sitting against the rock. She is going through the items in her wallet one by one.)*

Amoco card.

Amex. Master Card, soon to expire.

Driver's license. God, and people wonder why I hate getting my picture taken. *(Puts everything back in her wallet.)*

See, I'm trying very hard not to think about that piece of rock jutting out above my head. About half an hour ago, I noticed something very strange. I noticed it was covered with water, trickling out of that crack at the top. But the thing is — it's not, really. I know it's not. You'd have to be an idiot to believe that any kind of water out here is even a remote possibility, it's so freaking dry I can't even sweat anymore, I can hardly *blink.* It's obviously some kind of illusion. And that's why I haven't bothered getting up to check it — because I refuse to give in to wishful thinking. Because if I do, if I get up and start to desperately suck rock, I will have lost something crucial here. My dignity? No. It's more basic than that. My identity. I am a rational person, I know deep in the core of my animal brain that there are no miracles, there is no divine intervention, and there is no water. And the last thing I can do for myself, the last positive action I can take, is to not give in to false hope based on illusion.

But it's so damned *hard.* It's incredible what this heat can do to one's perceptions. For instance — I never really believed in mirages. I always thought they were something in the movies, like quicksand ... I mean, real to an extent, but not to the point of seeing palm trees or dancing girls or the Taj Mahal shimmering in the horizon. But they really do exist. Only out here, mirages don't look like water. They look like ice. Isn't that odd? It looks as if I'm surrounded by polar ice caps, fields of snow, sheets of blue crackling ice. And underneath, everything shimmers like ghosts, like it's all a memory of something that happened long ago.

See, if I let myself, I can actually see things from my past.

I'm serious. Look, over there ... I can see the broken sidewalk in front of our house in Providence, and the big oaks on either side. I can see snow falling over the Manhattan skyline the first winter I lived there. And I see blue. Blue, blue water.

45

What summer was that? My sixth? My seventh? I have on a big life jacket. I can feel the sun on my face, my knees tucked up tight to my chest ... drifting further and further away from shore until all I can see around me is ocean and water. And faraway voices so tiny, like insects on the horizon ... *(The faraway buzz of an airplane. She opens her eyes.)* What's that? *(Scans the sky.)*

What is it, am I starting to hear things now? Is that real? Is it real or am I making it up?

Oh God. Oh Jesus it's real it's real ... *(She fumbles through her dilly bag, emptying it onto the ground and scrabbling through the contents as the noise gets louder.)*

Christ, don't I have a mirror in here? A compact? Anything? Eye pencil, lip pencil ... shit! Help! I'm down here! Goddamn you, help me, I'm down here! *(She jumps up, pulling off her turban and waving it like a flag.)*

JESUS CHRIST, WHY DON'T YOU SEE ME? I'M RIGHT DOWN HERE! OPEN YOUR GODDAMN EYES AND NOTICE ME! *(Stops waving her shirt.)*

Fire. I've got to build a fire. Idiot, why didn't I think of that before? *(She crosses off and runs back on.)*

Shit! And there's no wood because there aren't any Goddamn trees! *(She crosses off and returns with some dead brush. She throws it down.)*

If they come back, they'll be able to see it. They should be able to see for miles ... *(She scrabbles through her bag, emptying it on the ground. Fishes out a pack of cigarettes and hurls them down.)*

No. No. Please dear God, don't tell me that today of all days I don't have any *matches? (She slams down her bag in frustration. She stares down at the trash by her feet; then she bends down and picks up a pair of reading glasses.)*

Jesus Christ, I am not going to die. *(She goes to the woodpile and tries to use one of the lenses to magnify sunlight.)* This has to work. There's so much sunlight, it just has to work.

Come on. Come on, you can do it. *(She continues trying to make a fire. The buzzing grows fainter and finally dies away completely. Alice continues working feverishly. She finally slams down her glasses in frustration and bursts into tears.)*

Fire fire everywhere, not a flame to drink. *(Wipes her face. She tastes her tears. She starts to ravenously wipe her face with her hands and licks them as she continues to weep silently. Lights shift. Lights up. It is dusk. The woodpile is untouched. Alice is huddled against the rock, her shirt wrapped around her.)*

Hey. I can see you.

Don't be so damn coy. Yes, you. Behind the rock.

You could at least come out so we can communicate properly. One on one.

Do you mind my asking a personal question? Why do they call you the "devil dingo"? Out of all the indigenous fauna, I'm sure there are others more devilish-looking than you. You're actually a fairly attractive species, as predators go.

Recognizable, at least. You might say, almost familiar. You remind me a little of old Spangle. She was half-spaniel, half-beagle, hence Spangle. Get it?

Jesus, I haven't thought of her in years.

So can I ask you bluntly? *Are* you actually the devil?

Because I don't believe in you, if you are. Nothing personal. For one thing, I know this is all a dream. I'm dreaming here. I just wanted to make that clear before this goes any further.

Was that you making all that racket a few minutes ago? Actually, there seems to be more than one of you, unless this hallucination is going further than I thought. A lot more of you, would be my guess. I'm not sure where you all are, exactly, but you seem to be getting closer.

Hey, I have a swell idea. I have part of a Power Bar that I'd love to share with you and your compadres. It's peanut butter-mocha, which you'll have to take my word for, is better than it sounds. Would you like the rest of it? *(Holds it out with difficulty.)* I can't throw it. If you want it, you're going to have to come and get it.

No?

I almost wish you *were* the devil. That way you could at least answer a few questions that have been bothering me. Like if this is hell, why am I so Goddamn cold? It feels like the temperature's dropped eighty degrees in the past hour. I'm freezing to death.

Are the ice caps closing in?

I wish you could take me around a little. Show me the sights. After all, this is all yours, isn't it? The landscape, I mean. The sky. This rock. According to my book, you made damn near everything around here, didn't you?

Hey, I just thought of something. If "God" is "dog" spelled backwards, then "dingo" spelled backwards is ... "ognid." *(Laughs. The sound of dingoes yapping.)*

Jesus.

Hey, was that you who made the water appear? You know. Out of the rock up there. That was a pretty neat trick, I must say. You'll have to explain how you did that to me some time. I bet it was you who turned the temperature down, too, wasn't it?

Can I ask you why?

You don't say. It was to make me feel better?

Well, that's damned thoughtful of you. I suppose I should thank you. Unfortunately, that reminds me of something I read somewhere. When a predator kills something, when a lion sinks its teeth into the neck of a gazelle, say, there's a sudden burst of endorphins in the dying animal. It's a final goodie, a last-second burst of pleasure, a bone nature throws you for being such a good little victim. Is that what you're doing?

Well, if it is, count me out. I don't want any of your pity. *(A dog growls.)* Oh Christ. Please, not yet.

Who are you, anyway? Are you God? Or are you the devil? Not that I honestly give a damn, because I don't. All I want to know is, do you have any pull here? Because I really don't want to die. Not out here, anyway. Not like this.

Look, I'm not going to lie to you. I don't have any illusions about who I am. I'm not a saint, and if truth be told, I'm not even especially nice. I'm middle-aged, middle-class, and middle of the road, and if you really took a hard look at my life, if you were really honest, I guess you could say I've blown it. I wasted it all on a career I stopped caring about years ago and a marriage I should have left but I didn't, and everything else, anything that could have meant something over the years, could have *defined* me, I methodically aborted and squashed down and talked myself out of one by one. I mean, I wanted to be a writer once upon a time. I wanted children, I wanted to fucking *travel*. But I'd always held everything back, everything I ever really wanted or thought or felt, to the point where I can't even remember what they are.

Now why did I do that?

I think I did it because — somewhere along the line — I got the idea that that's what I was *supposed* to be doing. That that's what being *good* was. And that somehow, secretly, you were watching me all along.

But were you? And if you were, did you honestly care? Did you ever care about any of it? *(The dog whimpers. Alice gets to her knees.)*

Look.

I'm groveling without irony. I'm actually *praying* for the first time in years, I don't even remember how the words go, I'm praying for my life.

I can't bargain with you. I'm not going to say I'm going to give you anything. For one thing, even with my smart-ass atheism, I really doubt it works that way. And besides, I honestly don't think I have anything you could possibly want. Because I don't have anything left. *(Upends her bag.)*

I mean, what. Money? You couldn't possibly want that. My identification, then? My credit? Any skin care products?

See? There's nothing. Nothing left at all. Just me and my shadow. All my flaws, my sins of omission. All my weaknesses and stubbornness and pride. *(Sound of barking, which subsides to a whimper.)*

What?

You don't mean that, do you. You actually want them? You're kidding, right?

Well. In that case, take my flaws. Please. Straight deal, even Steven. Just try not to spend them all in one place, OK? *(Leans back against the rock and shuts her eyes. The sound of whimpering dies down and then stops.)* Oh. And amen.

My mother used to come into my room every night to pray. She'd kneel next to me in the dark, and I'd mimic her. I'd put my hands together and bow my head down to the covers, and I'd repeat those mumbling words that seemed so strange. And invariably, the sound would wake Spangle from her doggy dreams beneath the bed ... and she'd creep over to me, and she'd nuzzle my hands with her cold, wet nose, and I'd hear the thump of her tail on the floor. And I'd kneel there, secretly stroking her soft muzzle, my mother next to me. And we'd pray. *(A beat. A faint light plays on her face.)*

How strange. I can almost hear something. A rumbling sound from far away. Is it the ice caps again?

Is it a car?

Or is it another illusion? *(The light grows brighter. Alice opens her eyes and stares straight out, waiting. The light grows impossibly bright. Lights slowly fade to black.)*

END OF PLAY

PROPERTY LIST

Guidebook
Camera
Watch
Compact
Bottle of water
Power Bar
Swiss army knife
Bottle of sunscreen
Painted cloth bag
Blouse
Sandal
Pebble
Wallet with credit cards and driver's license
Eye pencil
Lip pencil
Dead brush
Pack of cigarettes
Reading glasses

SOUND EFFECTS

Announcer's voice-over
Bus roaring away
Buzz of airplane
Dingoes yapping
Various dog sounds — growling, whimpering, barking

GOODBYE OSCAR

BY

ROMULUS LINNEY

GOODBYE OSCAR was produced by The Ensemble Studio Theatre (Curt Dempster, Artistic Director) at their Marathon '99, 22nd Annual Festival of New One-Act Plays, in New York City in May 1999. It was directed by Peter Maloney; the set design was by Kris Stone; the costume design was by Amela Baksic; the lighting design was by Greg MacPherson; the sound design was by Beatrice Terry; and the production stage manager was Gretchen Knowlton. The cast was as follows:

OSCAR . . . . Jack Gilpin
YOUNG GENTLEMAN . . . . Dashiell Eaves

CHARACTERS

OSCAR WILDE
YOUNG GENTLEMAN

SETTING

Hotel D'Alsace, Paris

TIME

November 30, 1900

GOODBYE OSCAR

English band music, but soft and distorted.

A table and two chairs. A coat tree with several coats, a hat, and a cane. A smaller table to one side, holding a tray, two glasses and a bottle of absinthe.

Oscar Wilde sits at the table, in shirtsleeves, back to us. A Young Gentleman enters. He is dressed in modern casual clothes.

YOUNG GENTLEMAN.   He says he is fighting a duel to the death with his wallpaper. He says he is dying beyond his means. His body is bloated and toxic. He is almost dead. Fever rises. Delirium, to wander in mind. He is young again. He thinks he leaves his bed in the Hotel D'Alsace *(The Young Gentleman takes a fur-lined overcoat from the rack, hands it to Oscar, who puts it on and walks about.)* He thinks he is wearing his fur-lined coat, watching in trains the great suns and moons of the United States of America. He thinks he arrives in Leadville, Colorado, where in fact, he did once lecture Americans on good taste. Again he admires miners, their clothes clean in the mornings, in their wide-brimmed hats, bandannas, boots and cloaks. He calls them the best-dressed men in America. *(The Young Gentleman escorts Oscar about.)* He goes again with a lecherous old man to a Leadville brothel. The ladies enjoy his accent and at the New Testament he recites in Greek, they laugh. But they listen to his poem about Jesus and the Whore.

OSCAR.   Your lovers are not dead I know, they will rise up and hear your voice and clash their cymbals and rejoice, and run to kiss your mouth, have no fear, only one God has ever died, only one God has ever let his side be pierced, by the soldier's spear. *(The Young Gentleman escorts Oscar back to his chair.)*

YOUNG GENTLEMAN. The old man tries to get Oscar drunk but Oscar outdrinks cowboys, never mind old men, and will not sleep with him. Very well, says the old man, being a good sport. He walks Oscar back to his hotel, arranges a treat for him. *(The Young Gentleman helps Oscar take off his coat.)* Don't go to bed yet, the old man says. Just wait. *(He leaves Oscar, who shrugs, takes off his jacket, sits and waits. The Young Gentleman goes to the coat tree, puts on the jacket of a poor bellhop. He becomes a young Boy, and knocks on an imaginary door.)*

OSCAR. Yes? Come in. *(Enter Boy. He has the tray, a bottle and two glasses.)*

BOY. Good evening!

OSCAR. Oh. Good evening.

BOY. May I join you? Oscar, right?

OSCAR. Yes. Did an old man send you?

BOY. Yes.

OSCAR. Did he tell you why?

BOY. He asked me to come in his place.

OSCAR. What do you think he meant?

BOY. Keep you company.

OSCAR. Would you enjoy that?

BOY. Sure.

OSCAR. Are you certain?

BOY. Yeah!

OSCAR. Well, then.

BOY. The old man said you liked absinthe.

OSCAR. I do. I'll pour. *(Oscar pours absinthe for them. The Boy takes off his hotel jacket and sits, waiting. Oscar hands him an absinthe.)* To your good health.

BOY. Yours. *(The Boy drinks, then chokes, coughs.)*

OSCAR. Sip. It's very strong.

BOY. Uh, yeah.

OSCAR. How much is the gentleman paying you?

BOY. Five dollars.

OSCAR. Oh, well then.

BOY. That's a lot of money! And everything's all right. Nobody knows I'm here.

OSCAR. I know you're here.

BOY. Don't you want me to be here?

OSCAR. At the moment I want to know why you are here.

BOY. That old man said you would like me.

OSCAR. And you would like me? Tell the truth.

BOY. I would like the five dollars.

OSCAR. Your eyes are red.

BOY. I've been rubbing them.

OSCAR. You've been crying.

BOY. Uh, yes.

OSCAR. Why?

BOY. I'd rather not say.

OSCAR. Five dollars.

BOY. Somebody died.

OSCAR. Who?

BOY. I lost a friend.

OSCAR. A waiter in the hotels or a bartender in the saloons or a cowboy on the plains? How old are you?

BOY. I'm thirty.

OSCAR. Please!

BOY. Twenty-five.

OSCAR. Please.

BOY. I'm sixteen.

OSCAR. I hear most cowboys die from pneumonia more than gunfights. They are just that, boys. Is it true?

BOY. I reckon.

OSCAR. You're not a cowboy yourself?

BOY. No.

OSCAR. What are you?

BOY. Not much.

OSCAR. Smile. Have you ever gone to bed with a man before?

BOY. Sure!

OSCAR. Let me put that another way. Have you ever gone to bed with anyone before?

BOY. Of course!

OSCAR. Make it ten dollars. And tell me the truth.

BOY. Women. Some.

OSCAR. Do you want to go to bed with me?

BOY. No.

OSCAR.   What do you want to do?

BOY.   Keep the ten dollars.

OSCAR.   You're in trouble.

BOY.   Yes.

OSCAR.   Are you afraid of someone?

BOY.   No.

OSCAR.   Steal something?

BOY.   No.

OSCAR.   Are you religious? Are you lamenting the crucifixion of Christ?

BOY.   No.

OSCAR.   Well, then. Is your heart broken?

BOY.   Yes.

OSCAR.   Do you need five more dollars to tell me why?

BOY.   You won't care.

OSCAR.   Who knows?

BOY.   My sister died.

OSCAR.   Really?

BOY.   We grew up together. Now she's gone.

OSCAR.   When?

BOY.   Three days ago.

OSCAR.   Was there a funeral?

BOY.   There was a burial.

OSCAR.   Did you cry then?

BOY.   No!

OSCAR.   You should have. I did.

BOY.   What?

OSCAR.   Cry. When my sister died. We must, you know.

BOY.   You had a sister who died?

OSCAR.   I was twelve. She was ten. *(Oscar takes a faded envelope from a pocket. It has childish scrawls and sketches of angels on it.)* In this envelope, which I keep with me always, is a lock of her hair. *(Oscar shows it to the Boy, then puts it on the table.)* Do you want to cry now?

BOY.   Yes.

OSCAR.   Why don't you?

BOY.   I'm working!

OSCAR.   For five dollars.

BOY. Ten, now!

OSCAR. To go to bed with me?

BOY. Yes!

OSCAR. Instead of crying about her?

BOY. Yes!

OSCAR. There is only one thing that matters. For those who really love, there is no help. None. We must do that for ourselves.

BOY. How?

OSCAR. Begin by crying.

BOY. What was your sister's name?

OSCAR. Isola. What was yours?

BOY. Sally.

OSCAR. To Sally and to Isola. Tread lightly, she is near, under the snow, speak gently, she can hear the flowers grow. All her bright golden hair, tarnished with rust, she that was young and fair, fallen to dust. Peace, peace, she cannot hear, lyre or sonnet, all my life's buried here, heap earth upon it. *(The Boy tries to hold back his grief.)*

BOY. What's a lyre?

OSCAR. A harp.

BOY. Oh. *(The Boy breaks down and weeps. Oscar waits a moment, then takes out a bill and puts it in the Boy's hand.)* This is a hundred dollars.

OSCAR. Good night.

BOY. Thank you. *(The Boy puts on his jacket.)* Thank you. You are a good and kind gentleman. I hope people always treat you the way you've treated me.

OSCAR. That is a very good line for an exit. I will remember it when I write a play.

BOY. Good night, sir. *(Oscar nods and sits staring ahead, drinking absinthe and looking at the envelope. Band music. The Boy goes to the coat tree and becomes the Young Gentleman. He changes his clothes.)*

YOUNG GENTLEMAN. Delirium, to wander in mind. Colorado and its suns and moons, the vast open United States dissolves into the steel confines of Reading Gaol, where as a convicted felon, as a foul corruptor of boys, he must soak thick rope in oakum tar, his hands bleeding, his ear split open and festering, his spirit destroyed by shame and humiliation. His only success was *Salome*, in Paris, which he never saw. It was the most shocking play ever taken from the scriptures, and the best. But now that fur-lined coat is on his mind. *(The Young Gentleman takes Oscar's fur-lined coat and replaces it with a shabby one. He puts it on Oscar.)* He lost it when he went into prison. He could never find another one like it when he came out, and he misses it, as his death rattle begins, as he lies the ex-convict, the morally impure abuser of youth, rash-ridden on a deathbed in the Hotel D'Alsace, dying beyond his means, fighting to the death with his wallpaper. *(We hear French children, voices distorted, singing "Sur le Pont D'Avignon." The Young Gentleman goes to the clothes tree. Oscar smiles, listening to the children, and he applauds them when they finish; they call out adieux to him. Oscar turns around and faces the Young Gentleman, now very properly dressed, in an elegant coat and vest, pearl-gray trousers, gloves, hat and cane. He is standing by the table. Band music.)*

YOUNG GENTLEMAN.   Good afternoon.

OSCAR.   Hello.

YOUNG GENTLEMAN.   Mr. Melmoth?

OSCAR.   Yes.

YOUNG GENTLEMAN.   What a pleasant day.

OSCAR.   Perfectly charming.

YOUNG GENTLEMAN.   Perhaps a little chilly.

OSCAR.   The children warm it up.

YOUNG GENTLEMAN.   They were singing for you?

OSCAR.   For the Queen of England. Today is her birthday. There's a band, and they were given a little party in her honor.

YOUNG GENTLEMAN.   By you.

OSCAR.   Tea and cake. A few tiny gifts children like. Children make me forget.

YOUNG GENTLEMAN.   Like a good cafe.

OSCAR.   This isn't a good cafe. It is fifth rate. With a very strange atmosphere, like something bizarre in a painting. But you seem intelligent. I approve that coat.

YOUNG GENTLEMAN.   I wanted to look my best.

OSCAR.   You are meeting someone important?

YOUNG GENTLEMAN.   Yes.

OSCAR. Enjoy your friendships. They are as important to us as parties are to children. Are you French?

YOUNG GENTLEMAN. No.

OSCAR. You certainly aren't English. American?

YOUNG GENTLEMAN. No.

OSCAR. You remind me of — oh, many young gentlemen I knew. But you are not being civil. You know my name. Tell me yours.

YOUNG GENTLEMAN. I am from the East.

OSCAR. No further questions, but this one, do you have any money?

YOUNG GENTLEMAN. Do you want a drink?

OSCAR. Yes, I *would* like a drink, yes.

YOUNG GENTLEMAN. Then you must have one. On me.

OSCAR. I am unable to return the favor.

YOUNG GENTLEMAN. Quite all right. *(The Young Gentleman takes up the absinthe bottle and two glasses, still on the table.)* You drink absinthe, I think.

OSCAR. Oh yes, absinthe, yes. I am very good company. *(The Young Gentleman pours out the green absinthe into the glasses.)*

YOUNG GENTLEMAN. I thought you might be.

OSCAR. Once, please believe this, I was thought the best dinner companion in the world. Now I sell its memory, the only currency I have. Of course, that was all in another country.

YOUNG GENTLEMAN. England? Cheers.

OSCAR. Cheers. *(They drink together.)* Ever been there?

YOUNG GENTLEMAN. Once or twice.

OSCAR. Did you like it?

YOUNG GENTLEMAN. Some of it.

OSCAR. But not all.

YOUNG GENTLEMAN. Definitely not all.

OSCAR. I can't go there anymore.

YOUNG GENTLEMAN. I like the lawns and the cheerfulness.

OSCAR. And the hard work.

YOUNG GENTLEMAN. And the carols.

OSCAR. Bookbinding.

YOUNG GENTLEMAN. First rate.

OSCAR. Music?

YOUNG GENTLEMAN. Some.

OSCAR. Architecture?

YOUNG GENTLEMAN. Not always.

OSCAR. Bit chilling.

YOUNG GENTLEMAN. Often.

OSCAR. They get so angry sometimes. They did at me.

YOUNG GENTLEMAN. Anger is not a productive state.

OSCAR. Are you an artist?

YOUNG GENTLEMAN. I do many things.

OSCAR. Artists make nothing good out of hatred. They must love the world, no matter what it does to them.

YOUNG GENTLEMAN. Or they to it.

OSCAR. That is exceedingly well-put.

YOUNG GENTLEMAN. Thank you.

OSCAR. I must say, you make me recall something I have not felt for a long time.

YOUNG GENTLEMAN. What?

OSCAR. Encouragement.

YOUNG GENTLEMAN. I knew of a gentleman once who encouraged others. All the time. Would you like to hear about him?

OSCAR. Gladly.

YOUNG GENTLEMAN. This gentleman was very eloquent. He talked about Art.

OSCAR. Oh. I hope he wasn't tiresome.

YOUNG GENTLEMAN. No, he wasn't. He said there is no need to talk about reality. That just happens. But we must talk about Art, so it will exist. Otherwise, we kill it. And that is a profound tragedy, since nature is always reproducing itself for its survival, but every real work of art is unique, created by one single person, who will never come again. He illustrated this notion by telling stories about Jesus Christ, of all people, whom he considered not God but a perfectly realized and very great Artist, whose Art was his life. In one of his stories Christ comes across a drunken sinner, with roses in his hair, his lips red with wine, and says to him, "My friend, why do you live like this?" And the sinner says, "I was a leper. You healed me. I was so miserable then, I must be happy now."

OSCAR. Ah, yes. Then Christ saw a woman with another sinner following her, and Christ said, "My friend, why are you looking at that woman that way?" And the sinner said, "I was blind and you healed me. What else should I do with my eyes?"

YOUNG GENTLEMAN. And Christ saw a third man, crying, and he said, "My friend, why are you crying?" And the third man said, "I was dead, and you brought me back to life. What else should I do in this life but cry?"

OSCAR. Then Christ was very sad. He went and sat next to his Father in Heaven, where all these sinners stood naked in the Judgement Hall of God. *(They are both telling these stories now, with relish.)*

YOUNG GENTLEMAN. "You have lived an evil life," said God the Father to a fourth sinner. "I must send you to hell."

OSCAR. "You can't," said the fourth sinner.

YOUNG GENTLEMAN. "Why not?" said God.

OSCAR. "Because I always lived there," said the fourth sinner. And there was silence in the Judgement Hall of God.

YOUNG GENTLEMAN. And Christ said to God, "Well, since you can't send him to hell, send him to heaven."

OSCAR. "He can't do that either," said the fourth sinner.

YOUNG GENTLEMAN. "Why not?" said Christ.

OSCAR. "Because I have no Art, and without Art, I cannot imagine heaven."

YOUNG GENTLEMAN. And Christ said to a fifth sinner, "Are you an artist, too?" And the fifth sinner said, "Yes," and Christ said to the fifth sinner, "How do you imagine God's heaven with your Art?"

OSCAR. The fifth sinner said, "I am a sculptor. My wife died. I was desolate, and deathly ill. I made a statue of myself mourning over her tomb. I called it *The Sorrow That Lasts Forever.* But it did not help. I thought I would go mad with grief. Nothing made any sense. So I broke it up. I made a statue of a dancer. I put it by the tomb, and I called it *The Pleasure That Lasts for a Moment.* And I saw heaven."

YOUNG GENTLEMAN. And there was a great silence in the Judgement Hall of God.

OSCAR.   Did we know each other? I don't remember telling you my stories anywhere.

YOUNG GENTLEMAN.   I was there, where you were. I did that too, upon occasion. Tell stories, I mean.

OSCAR.   Why did you listen to mine?

YOUNG GENTLEMAN.   Like the sculptor who thinks in bronze, I think in stories. So do you.

OSCAR.   That is absolutely true. Who are you?

YOUNG GENTLEMAN.   Someone like you. *(A band softly plays "God Save the Queen," the American "My Country Tis of Thee." Oscar stands staring, stricken but not showing it. The Young Gentleman drinks his absinthe. The music ends.)* That is what they took away from you.

OSCAR.   Yes. Well.

YOUNG GENTLEMAN.   They don't like you.

OSCAR.   No.

YOUNG GENTLEMAN.   I do, though. More?

OSCAR.   Please! *(The Young Gentleman pours.)* You are a very curious gentleman.

YOUNG GENTLEMAN.   So are you.

OSCAR.   My name is not Melmoth.

YOUNG GENTLEMAN.   I know what your name is. Cheers.

OSCAR.   Cheers. *(They drink together.)* Really, we must have met. I do seem to remember you from somewhere.

YOUNG GENTLEMAN.   We've seen each other about. You with another young man.

OSCAR.   You've seen him? Here?

YOUNG GENTLEMAN.   Very beautiful, and very wicked.

OSCAR.   Do you know where he is now?

YOUNG GENTLEMAN.   I do.

OSCAR.   WHERE? Sorry. I raised my voice. That is what he does to me.

YOUNG GENTLEMAN.   I understand.

OSCAR.   I still love him.

YOUNG GENTLEMAN.   But does he love you?

OSCAR.   He tries. He comes to see me, then gets bored. I have no money. He calls me an old whore, and leaves me.

YOUNG GENTLEMAN.   He won't do it again.

OSCAR. No?

YOUNG GENTLEMAN. He inherited a fortune. He's raising horses.

OSCAR. Horses?

YOUNG GENTLEMAN. Um. Do you still love him?

OSCAR. Forever.

YOUNG GENTLEMAN. In spite of what he did to you?

OSCAR. Or because of it. Do you understand what it is to be betrayed?

YOUNG GENTLEMAN. It is a part of my charm, as it will be of yours.

OSCAR. Then you've been betrayed, too?

YOUNG GENTLEMAN. Once.

OSCAR. You loved as strongly as I did?

YOUNG GENTLEMAN. Oh, yes.

OSCAR. Who?

YOUNG GENTLEMAN. You, among others. I am very promiscuous that way.

OSCAR. And were you betrayed as I was?

YOUNG GENTLEMAN. I told you, once. But that once was spectacular.

OSCAR. I am very drunk. This absinthe. You are so charming, well, are you Jesus Christ?

YOUNG GENTLEMAN. I am.

OSCAR. This is absurd. Really?

YOUNG GENTLEMAN. Positively, none other, I assure you.

OSCAR. It would be just like me, when I lie dying, to presume I meet you, have known you somewhere before, when I loved the gospels at Oxford, or perhaps here and there, some young man who looked like you.

YOUNG GENTLEMAN. Does it matter, if it's me?

OSCAR. No. In that case, how do you do?

YOUNG GENTLEMAN. Very well, thank you.

OSCAR. Why are you here, waiting for me?

YOUNG GENTLEMAN. As the Artist on his deathbed sees heaven, you see me.

OSCAR. On my deathbed?

YOUNG GENTLEMAN. Yes.

OSCAR. Oh. Am I dead yet?

YOUNG GENTLEMAN. Not quite.

OSCAR. I hate to seem inquisitive, but when do I die?

YOUNG GENTLEMAN. When you stop dreaming.

OSCAR. You're being obscure. I see you quite clearly. We sit, talk. Dreams jump about.

YOUNG GENTLEMAN. Not the last one. Death you of all men see as a story. This is your last story.

OSCAR. Meeting Jesus in a fifth rate cafe, is that a good story?

YOUNG GENTLEMAN. I like it.

OSCAR. Is this all there is to it?

YOUNG GENTLEMAN. A friend will call a priest. You will raise your hand, and be received into the church. All perfectly natural. Another? *(The Young Gentleman pours Oscar another absinthe.)*

OSCAR. Thank you so much. *(The Young Gentleman pours. They drink.)* What will happen to my sons?

YOUNG GENTLEMAN. One will try to forget you. He will be a soldier, die bravely in war. The other will remember you, live a long time, have a son of his own, who will have a son. They will write loving books about you.

OSCAR. And I? *(The Young Gentleman gets up, stands behind Oscar, with his hands on Oscar's shoulders.)*

YOUNG GENTLEMAN. You will die in a fifth-rate hotel, like this cafe. That's where you are now. Only a few friends are with you, but they are doing their best. The owner of the poor hotel holds you in his arms. So do I.

OSCAR. Why does he care? Why should Jesus Christ care about Oscar Wilde?

YOUNG GENTLEMAN. Wouldn't it be boring if I came for the righteous?

OSCAR. It would be tedious.

YOUNG GENTLEMAN. Should not those who love more than most, be forgiven more than most?

OSCAR. That is perfectly charming. *(Oscar coughs.)* Oh! *(He gasps.)*

YOUNG GENTLEMAN. It will only be a moment.

OSCAR. I — can't — breathe!

68

YOUNG GENTLEMAN. Then don't. *(Oscar dies, then breathes freely again.)*

OSCAR. I feel so much better!

YOUNG GENTLEMAN. Are you quite ready?

OSCAR. Whenever you are.

YOUNG GENTLEMAN. Then we'll go. *(The Young Gentleman hands Oscar his hat and cane.)* Would you like to say goodbye?

OSCAR. I beg your pardon? *(The Young Gentleman indicates the audience.)*

YOUNG GENTLEMAN. To the future.

OSCAR. Oh. Yes. *(Band music. The Young Gentleman nods, steps back, and waits. To us.)* I lost my friends in life, but I hope to make new ones after death. I do so want you to be among them. You can easily find me. Where there is laughter, and pleasure, there is truth. There I will wait for you. Good night. *(The Young Gentleman holds out Oscar's hat and cane for him. Oscar puts on his hat and prepares himself. The Young Gentleman waits for Oscar to join him. Oscar does and as the band plays softly, Oscar goes with the Young Gentleman into Paradise.)*

END OF PLAY

PROPERTY LIST

Tray
Bottle of absinthe
Two glasses

Fur-lined overcoat (YOUNG GENTLEMAN)
Bellhop jacket (YOUNG GENTLEMAN)
Faded envelope with drawings on it (OSCAR)
Hundred-dollar bill (OSCAR)
Shabby coat (YOUNG GENTLEMAN)

SOUND EFFECTS

English band music
Children singing "Sur le Pont D'Avignon"
Children calling out "adieu"

NEW PLAYS

★ **MATCH by Stephen Belber.** Mike and Lisa Davis interview a dancer and choreographer about his life, but it is soon evident that their agenda will either ruin or inspire them—and definitely change their lives forever. "Prolific laughs and ear-to-ear smiles." —*NY Magazine*. "Uproariously funny, deeply moving, enthralling theater. Stephen Belber's MATCH has great beauty and tenderness, and abounds in wit." —*NY Daily News*. "Three and a half out of four stars." —*USA Today*. "A theatrical steeplechase that leads straight from outrageous bitchery to unadorned, heartfelt emotion." —*Wall Street Journal*. [2M, 1W] ISBN: 0-8222-2020-2

★ **HANK WILLIAMS: LOST HIGHWAY by Randal Myler and Mark Harelik.** The story of the beloved and volatile country-music legend Hank Williams, featuring twenty-five of his most unforgettable songs. "[LOST HIGHWAY has] the exhilarating feeling of Williams on stage in a particular place on a particular night…serves up classic country with the edges raw and the energy hot…By the end of the play, you've traveled on a profound emotional journey: LOST HIGHWAY transports its audience and communicates the inspiring message of the beauty and richness of Williams' songs…forceful, clear-eyed, moving, impressive." —*Rolling Stone*. "…honors a very particular musical talent with care and energy…smart, sweet, poignant." —*NY Times*. [7M, 3W] ISBN: 0-8222-1985-9

★ **THE STORY by Tracey Scott Wilson.** An ambitious black newspaper reporter goes against her editor to investigate a murder and finds the *best* story…but at what cost? "A singular new voice…deeply emotional, deeply intellectual, and deeply musical…" —*The New Yorker*. "…a conscientious and absorbing new drama…" —*NY Times*. "…a riveting, tough-minded drama about race, reporting and the truth…" —*A.P.* "…a stylish, attention-holding script that ends on a chilling note that will leave viewers with much to talk about." —*Curtain Up*. [2M, 7W (doubling, flexible casting)] ISBN: 0-8222-1998-0

★ **OUR LADY OF 121st STREET by Stephen Adly Guirgis.** The body of Sister Rose, beloved Harlem nun, has been stolen, reuniting a group of life-challenged childhood friends who square off as they wait for her return. "A scorching and dark new comedy… Mr. Guirgis has one of the finest imaginations for dialogue to come along in years." —*NY Times*. "Stephen Guirgis may be the best playwright in America under forty." —*NY Magazine*. [8M, 4W] ISBN: 0-8222-1965-4

★ **HOLLYWOOD ARMS by Carrie Hamilton and Carol Burnett.** The coming-of-age story of a dreamer who manages to escape her bleak life and follow her romantic ambitions to stardom. Based on Carol Burnett's bestselling autobiography, *One More Time*. "…pure theatre and pure entertainment…" —*Talkin' Broadway*. "…a warm, fuzzy evening of theatre." —*BroadwayBeat.com*. "…chuckles and smiles of recognition or surprise flow naturally…a remarkable slice of life." —*TheatreScene.net*. [5M, 5W, 1 girl] ISBN: 0-8222-1959-X

★ **INVENTING VAN GOGH by Steven Dietz.** A haunting and hallucinatory drama about the making of art, the obsession to create and the fine line that separates truth from myth. "Like a van Gogh painting, Dietz's story is a gorgeous example of excess—one that remakes reality with broad, well-chosen brush strokes. At evening's end, we're left with the author's resounding opinions on art and artifice, and provoked by his constant query into which is greater: van Gogh's art or his violent myth." —*Phoenix New Times*. "Dietz's writing is never simple. It is always brilliant. Shaded, compressed, direct, lucid—he frames his subject with a remarkable understanding of painting as a physical experience." —*Tucson Citizen*. [4M, 1W] ISBN: 0-8222-1954-9

DRAMATISTS PLAY SERVICE, INC.
440 Park Avenue South, New York, NY 10016 212-683-8960 Fax 212-213-1539
postmaster@dramatists.com www.dramatists.com

NEW PLAYS

★ **INTIMATE APPAREL by Lynn Nottage.** The moving and lyrical story of a turn-of-the-century black seamstress whose gifted hands and sewing machine are the tools she uses to fashion her dreams from the whole cloth of her life's experiences. "...Nottage's play has a delicacy and eloquence that seem absolutely right for the time she is depicting..." *–NY Daily News.* "...thoughtful, affecting...The play offers poignant commentary on an era when the cut and color of one's dress—and of course, skin—determined whom one could and could not marry, sleep with, even talk to in public." *–Variety.* [2M, 4W] ISBN: 0-8222-2009-1

★ **BROOKLYN BOY by Donald Margulies.** A witty and insightful look at what happens to a writer when his novel hits the bestseller list. "The characters are beautifully drawn, the dialogue sparkles..." *–nytheatre.com.* "Few playwrights have the mastery to smartly investigate so much through a laugh-out-loud comedy that combines the vintage subject matter of successful writer-returning-to-ethnic-roots with the familiar mid-life crisis." *–Show Business Weekly.* [4M, 3W] ISBN: 0-8222-2074-1

★ **CROWNS by Regina Taylor.** Hats become a springboard for an exploration of black history and identity in this celebratory musical play. "Taylor pulls off a Hat Trick: She scores thrice, turning CROWNS into an artful amalgamation of oral history, fashion show, and musical theater..." *–TheatreMania.com.* "...wholly theatrical...Ms. Taylor has created a show that seems to arise out of spontaneous combustion, as if a bevy of department-store customers simultaneously decided to stage a revival meeting in the changing room." *–NY Times.* [1M, 6W (2 musicians)] ISBN: 0-8222-1963-8

★ **EXITS AND ENTRANCES by Athol Fugard.** The story of a relationship between a young playwright on the threshold of his career and an aging actor who has reached the end of his. "[Fugard] can say more with a single line than most playwrights convey in an entire script...Paraphrasing the title, it's safe to say this drama, making its memorable entrance into our consciousness, is unlikely to exit as long as a theater exists for exceptional work." *–Variety.* "A thought-provoking, elegant and engrossing new play..." *–Hollywood Reporter.* [2M] ISBN: 0-8222-2041-5

★ **BUG by Tracy Letts.** A thriller featuring a pair of star-crossed lovers in an Oklahoma City motel facing a bug invasion, paranoia, conspiracy theories and twisted psychological motives. "...obscenely exciting...top-flight craftsmanship. Buckle up and brace yourself..." *–NY Times.* "...[a] thoroughly outrageous and thoroughly entertaining play...the possibility of enemies, real and imagined, to squash has never been more theatrical." *–A.P.* [3M, 2W] ISBN: 0-8222-2016-4

★ **THOM PAIN (BASED ON NOTHING) by Will Eno.** An ordinary man muses on childhood, yearning, disappointment and loss, as he draws the audience into his last-ditch plea for empathy and enlightenment. "It's one of those treasured nights in the theater—treasured nights anywhere, for that matter—that can leave you both breathless with exhilaration and...in a puddle of tears." *–NY Times.* "Eno's words...are familiar, but proffered in a way that is constantly contradictory to our expectations. Beckett is certainly among his literary ancestors." *–nytheatre.com.* [1M] ISBN: 0-8222-2076-8

★ **THE LONG CHRISTMAS RIDE HOME by Paula Vogel.** Past, present and future collide on a snowy Christmas Eve for a troubled family of five. "...[a] lovely and hauntingly original family drama...a work that breathes so much life into the theater." *–Time Out.* "...[a] delicate visual feast..." *–NY Times.* "...brutal and lovely...the overall effect is magical." *–NY Newsday.* [3M, 3W] ISBN: 0-8222-2003-2

DRAMATISTS PLAY SERVICE, INC.
440 Park Avenue South, New York, NY 10016 212-683-8960 Fax 212-213-1539
postmaster@dramatists.com   www.dramatists.com